Hammerhead Sharks

by Rebecca Pettiford

BELLWETHER MEDIA • MINNEAPOLIS, MN

Blastoff! Readers are carefully developed by literacy experts to build reading stamina and move students toward fluency by combining standards-based content with developmentally appropriate text.

Level 1 provides the most support through repetition of high-frequency words, light text, predictable sentence patterns, and strong visual support.

Level 2 offers early readers a bit more challenge through varied sentences, increased text load, and text-supportive special features.

Level 3 advances early-fluent readers toward fluency through increased text load, less reliance on photos, advancing concepts, longer sentences, and more complex special features.

★ **Blastoff! Universe**

Reading Level

Grade **K**

Grades **1–3**

Grade **4**

This edition first published in 2021 by Bellwether Media, Inc.

No part of this publication may be reproduced in whole or in part without written permission of the publisher. For information regarding permission, write to Bellwether Media, Inc., Attention: Permissions Department, 6012 Blue Circle Drive, Minnetonka, MN 55343.

Library of Congress Cataloging-in-Publication Data

Names: Pettiford, Rebecca, author.
Title: Hammerhead sharks / by Rebecca Pettiford.
Description: Minneapolis, MN : Bellwether Media, [2021] | Series: Blastoff! Readers: Shark frenzy | Includes bibliographical references and index. | Audience: Ages 5-8 | Audience: Grades 2-3 | Summary: "Simple text and full-color photography introduce beginning readers to hammerhead sharks. Developed by literacy experts for students in kindergarten through third grade"– Provided by publisher.
Identifiers: LCCN 2020001615 (print) | LCCN 2020001616 (ebook) | ISBN 9781644872468 (library binding) | ISBN 9781681037097 (ebook)
Subjects: LCSH: Hammerhead sharks–Juvenile literature.
Classification: LCC QL638.95.S7 P48 2021 (print) | LCC QL638.95.S7 (ebook) | DDC 597.3/4–dc23
LC record available at https://lccn.loc.gov/2020001615
LC ebook record available at https://lccn.loc.gov/2020001616

Table of Contents

cephalofoil

great hammerhead shark

Hammerhead sharks have flat, hammer-shaped heads. This special head shape is called a **cephalofoil**.

Hammerhead sharks live in **shallow** waters all over the world. They are found in coastal areas and along **continental shelves**.

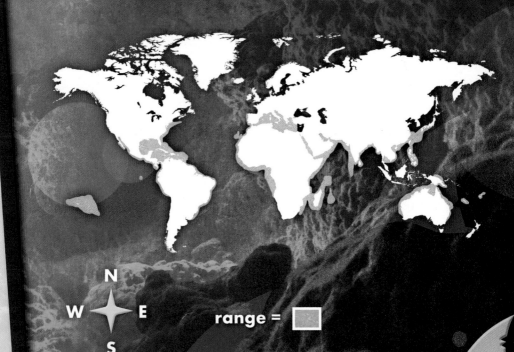

Great Hammerhead Shark Range

N
W E
S

range =

5

There are ten **species** of hammerhead sharks. The smallest is 35 inches (89 centimeters) long. But great hammerheads grow up to 20 feet (6 meters) long!

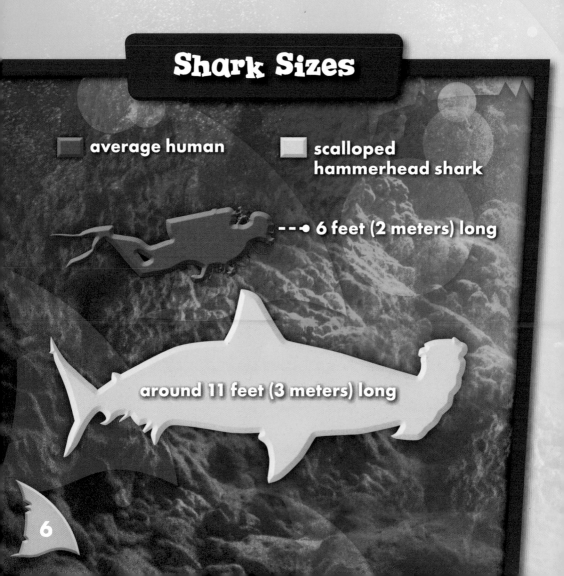

Shark Sizes

average human

scalloped hammerhead shark

6 feet (2 meters) long

around 11 feet (3 meters) long

scalloped
hammerhead
shark

Some species are overfished.
People are trying to save
hammerheads by setting
controls on fishing.

Head Hunters

smooth hammerhead shark

Hammerheads have an eye at each end of their heads. This allows the sharks to see all around them.

Their cephalofoil helps them spot **prey**. It also helps them get away from **predators**.

All sharks have **sensors**. Hammerheads have more sensors than other sharks.

Identify a Hammerhead Shark

dorsal fin

cephalofoil

dark-colored back

The sensors are spread out on the underside of their heads. They help the sharks easily find food.

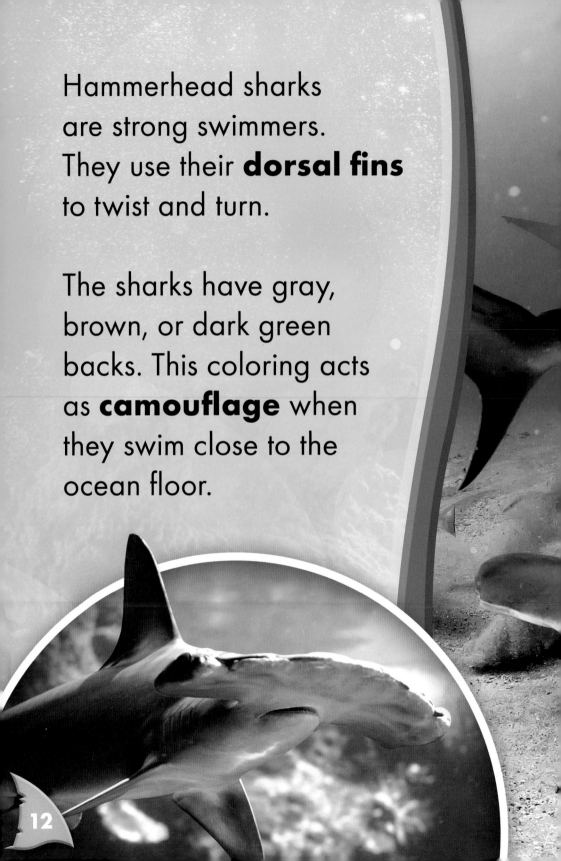

Hammerhead sharks are strong swimmers. They use their **dorsal fins** to twist and turn.

The sharks have gray, brown, or dark green backs. This coloring acts as **camouflage** when they swim close to the ocean floor.

dorsal fin

Hammerheads are **carnivores**. They eat stingrays, squids, and fish.

Some species use their heads like clubs to strike prey. Then they use their sharp teeth to tear food apart!

Hammerhead Shark Diet

fish

stingrays

squids

Hammerhead sharks hunt at night. They prowl shallow waters looking for food. Some hunt alone while others hunt in groups.

The sharks may **migrate** over 750 miles (1,207 kilometers) to look for food.

Hammerheads do not have many predators. But they have to watch out for great white sharks and **orcas**. People are threats, too.

These sharks are **unique** members of the ocean world!

19

Deep Dive on the Great Hammerhead Shark

LIFE SPAN:
around 30 years

LENGTH:
up to 20 feet
(6 meters) long

WEIGHT:
up to 1,000 pounds (454 kilograms)

TOP SPEED:
around 25 miles
(40 kilometers) per hour

DEPTH RANGE:
up to 984 feet (300 meters)

dark-colored
back

dorsal fin

cephalofoil

conservation status: critically endangered

Glossary

camouflage—a way of using color to blend in with surroundings

carnivores—animals that only eat meat

cephalofoil—the hammer or wing-like shape of a hammerhead shark's head

continental shelves—the edges of large areas of land that lie under the ocean and slope down to the ocean floor

dorsal fins—fins at the top of a hammerhead shark's back

migrate—to move from one area to another, often with the seasons

orcas—killer whales

predators—animals that hunt other animals for food

prey—animals that are hunted by other animals for food

sensors—body parts that sense movement, heat, light, or sound

shallow—not deep

species—groups of animals or plants that are similar and can reproduce

unique—one of a kind

To Learn More

AT THE LIBRARY

Alderman, Christine Thomas. *Hammerhead Sharks*. Mankato, Minn.: Black Rabbit Books, 2020.

Morey, Allan. *Hammerhead Sharks*. Mankato, Minn.: Amicus High Interest, 2017.

Twiddy, Robin. *Hammerhead Shark*. New York, N.Y.: Greenhaven Publishing, 2020.

ON THE WEB

FACTSURFER

Factsurfer.com gives you a safe, fun way to find more information.

1. Go to www.factsurfer.com.

2. Enter "hammerhead sharks" into the search box and click 🔍.

3. Select your book cover to see a list of related content.

Index